The Power of No

The Power of No

Matthew Petchinsky

1

The Power of No: How to Set Boundaries and Get Rich

By: Matthew Petchinsky

Disclaimer

This book, *The Power of No: How to Set Boundaries and Get Rich*, is intended for **educational, informational, and inspirational purposes only**. It is not a substitute for professional financial, legal, medical, psychological, or therapeutic advice. The author is not acting as a licensed financial advisor, investment professional, attorney, physician, therapist, or mental health provider.

All concepts, strategies, examples, and reflections presented in this book are designed to encourage **personal awareness, boundary development, and mindset shifts** related to time, energy, labor, and decision-making. Any financial references—including income, wealth, success, or economic outcomes—are **illustrative only** and should not be interpreted as guarantees of financial results. Individual outcomes will vary based on personal circumstances, effort, experience, market conditions, and external factors beyond the author's control.

Nothing in this book should be construed as financial advice, investment guidance, tax strategy, or a recommendation to engage in or avoid any specific business, employment, or financial activity. Readers are strongly encouraged to consult qualified professionals before making significant financial, legal, or career decisions.

This book also addresses **emotional boundaries, interpersonal dynamics, and personal empowerment**. While these topics may overlap with areas commonly discussed in therapy or counseling, this book does not diagnose, treat, or cure any mental health condition. If you are experiencing emotional distress, trauma, anxiety, depression, or relationship abuse, seek support from a licensed mental health professional or appropriate support services.

The practice of setting boundaries—including saying "no" to people, opportunities, obligations, or systems—may result in **emotional discomfort, interpersonal conflict, social pushback, or changes**

in relationships. The author assumes no responsibility for personal, professional, or relational outcomes that may arise from applying the ideas discussed in this book. Readers are solely responsible for how they choose to implement these concepts.

Any stories, scenarios, or examples included in this book are either fictionalized, anonymized, composite representations, or generalized illustrations meant to convey principles rather than depict real individuals or situations. Any resemblance to actual persons, living or dead, or real events is purely coincidental.

By reading this book, you acknowledge that **personal growth, boundary enforcement, and financial improvement involve risk, responsibility, and self-reflection**, and that no outcome is guaranteed. You accept full responsibility for your choices, actions, and results.

This book does not promote illegal activity, exploitation, manipulation, coercion, or harm to others. The principles discussed are intended to support **ethical self-advocacy, personal sovereignty, and sustainable success**.

If you do not agree with or accept these terms, you should discontinue reading this book.

Introduction: The Wealth in Saying No

Most people are taught that wealth comes from saying *yes*.

Yes to overtime.
Yes to unpaid favors.
Yes to emotional labor.
Yes to being available, agreeable, flexible, accommodating, and endlessly understanding.

Yes to burning out quietly.

But almost no one teaches the truth:

Wealth begins the moment you learn to say no without guilt.

This book is not about becoming selfish.
It is about becoming **sovereign**.

Because poverty is rarely just a lack of money—it is a chronic **leak of energy, time, attention, and self-trust**. And those leaks almost always come from weak or violated boundaries.

Every unwanted obligation drains capital.
Every unspoken resentment compounds interest.
Every "yes" spoken out of fear steals from your future.

Saying no is not a rejection of opportunity.
It is a **filter for alignment**.

The Hidden Cost of Yes

Most financial advice focuses on income streams, investments, and hustle. But few ask the more dangerous question:

Where is your money bleeding out through your boundaries?

- Staying in underpaid roles because you don't want to disappoint
- Supporting others financially at the expense of your own stability
- Overworking to earn approval instead of value
- Saying yes to projects that exhaust you but don't advance you
- Allowing emotional manipulation to dictate your financial decisions

These patterns don't just limit wealth—they **train your nervous system to associate money with fear, obligation, and self-erasure**.

This is why so many people work harder every year yet feel poorer, more trapped, and more exhausted.

They are earning—but they are not protected.

Boundaries Are a Wealth Technology

A boundary is not a wall.
It is a **gate**.
It decides:

- What enters your life
- What drains you
- What you invest in
- What you refuse to subsidize

Every financially stable person—whether consciously or not—has mastered selective refusal.

They know:

- Not every opportunity deserves access
- Not every request is reasonable
- Not every relationship earns proximity
- Not every emergency is theirs to solve

They are not cruel.
They are **clear**.
And clarity compounds.

Why "No" Feels So Dangerous

If saying no feels terrifying, it's not because you're weak.
It's because you were conditioned.

Many people were trained—by family systems, workplaces, culture, or survival circumstances—that love, safety, or acceptance depended on compliance. That saying no would result in rejection, punishment, or abandonment.

So the nervous system learned a lie:

Saying no is unsafe.

This book gently but firmly dismantles that lie.

Because the truth is this:

What feels unsafe is often the doorway to wealth.

Not just financial wealth—but:

- Emotional stability
- Time ownership
- Creative freedom
- Decision clarity
- Self-respect

Money follows those who are internally regulated enough to protect themselves.

Rich Is Not Loud—It Is Protected

This book does not promise overnight riches or manipulative tactics. It offers something far more powerful and sustainable:

A recalibration of your relationship with power.

Real wealth is quiet.
It sleeps at night.
It does not explain itself.
It does not overextend.
It does not beg.

Wealth moves *away* from chaos.

And chaos thrives wherever boundaries collapse.

What This Book Will Teach You

In the pages ahead, you will learn how to:

- Identify where your "yes" is costing you money
- Recognize financial manipulation disguised as obligation
- Separate generosity from self-betrayal
- Build boundary systems that protect income and energy
- Say no without overexplaining, justifying, or collapsing
- Rewire guilt, fear, and people-pleasing around money
- Create wealth by subtraction, not exhaustion

You will learn that saying no is not the end of connection—it is the beginning of **respect**.

A New Definition of Rich

By the end of this book, "rich" will no longer mean:

- Always available
- Constantly striving
- Emotionally overdrawn
- Financially reactive

Instead, it will mean:

- Selective
- Grounded
- Protected
- Calm
- Self-directed

Rich is having the power to decline without panic.
Rich is choosing alignment over approval.
Rich is knowing that every no creates space for a higher yes.

This is not a book about denial.

It is a book about **ownership**.

And it starts with the most underestimated word in the language:

No.

Welcome to *The Power of No.*

Chapter 1: Why "Yes" Is Keeping You Broke and Stressed

Time Leaks: The Silent Thief of Wealth

Time is the only asset you spend before you earn it, yet it is the one most commonly given away without intention. Every unnecessary meeting, unpaid favor, last-minute request, or obligation accepted out of guilt quietly drains hours that could have been invested into income, rest, learning, or growth. When time leaks accumulate, they do not just delay progress—they create chronic urgency, forcing you to operate in reaction mode rather than strategy mode. This constant scrambling erodes your ability to plan, evaluate opportunities, and negotiate from strength. Over time, the absence of protected time becomes a financial ceiling you cannot break through, no matter how hard you work.

Many people believe being busy is proof of productivity, but busyness often masks inefficiency caused by unfiltered access to your availability. Saying yes too often teaches others that your time is endlessly expandable, even when it is not. This creates a dynamic where you are always behind, always catching up, and always overcommitted. The stress that follows is not a personal failure—it is the predictable outcome of unmanaged time boundaries. Wealth requires margin, and margin cannot exist where time is constantly leaking.

Time leaks are especially dangerous because they feel harmless in isolation. One favor here, one extra task there, one more responsibility added without removing another. Over months and years, these small yeses compound into exhaustion and stagnation. You may feel like you are always working yet never advancing, always busy yet financially stuck. This is not because you lack discipline, but because your time has been fragmented beyond its capacity to generate momentum.

Learning to identify time leaks is the first step toward reclaiming control. When you recognize that every yes consumes a finite resource, you begin to treat your schedule as a financial instrument rather than an emotional one. Time protected becomes time invested. Time invested becomes leverage. And leverage is the foundation of sustainable wealth.

Energy Drains: When Effort Exceeds Return

Energy is the currency that determines how effectively your time is used. Two people can spend the same number of hours working and produce radically different results based on how depleted or supported they feel. Saying yes to tasks, environments, and people that drain you emotionally or mentally reduces the quality of your output. When energy is constantly depleted, creativity shrinks, decision-making weakens, and resilience collapses under pressure. This leads to working harder for diminishing returns.

Chronic energy drains often come from obligations that are misaligned with your values or strengths. You may say yes because you feel responsible, needed, or afraid of disappointing someone. Yet each time you override your internal signals, your nervous system learns that your needs are negotiable. This creates a cycle of burnout followed by recovery, followed by burnout again, with no upward financial trajectory. Exhaustion becomes normalized, even glorified, while progress remains elusive.

Energy drains are frequently misinterpreted as motivation problems. In reality, they are boundary problems. When your energy is siphoned into emotionally taxing situations or low-impact work, you lose access to sustained focus and clarity. Stress hormones remain elevated, making it harder to think long-term or assess opportunities accurately. Financial decisions made from depletion are often reactive, defensive, and rooted in fear rather than strategy.

Protecting your energy is not indulgent; it is essential. Wealth is built through consistent, high-quality effort applied in the right places. When you begin to say no to what drains you, you create space for work that energizes and compounds. Energy conserved becomes energy invested, and energy invested wisely multiplies rather than depletes.

Emotional Labor Subsidies: Paying for Others with Your Life

Emotional labor becomes a financial issue when you repeatedly absorb stress, responsibility, and problem-solving for others without compensation or reciprocity. This often shows up as being the fixer, the listener, the peacemaker, or the reliable one. You may manage other people's emotions, smooth conflicts, or carry unspoken expectations simply to maintain harmony. While this may feel necessary, it quietly taxes your mental and emotional reserves.

When emotional labor is unacknowledged or unpaid, it functions as a subsidy. You are covering costs that should belong to someone else. Over time, this reduces your capacity to focus on your own goals, opportunities, and financial stability. The stress generated by carrying emotional weight spills into your work life, affecting concentration, confidence, and negotiation power. Money stagnates when emotional labor dominates your bandwidth.

This pattern is often reinforced by messages about being supportive, selfless, or "the strong one." Obligation becomes framed as virtue, while boundaries are framed as selfishness. As a result, you may feel responsible for maintaining systems that actively drain you. This creates resentment, guilt, and exhaustion—none of which are conducive to wealth creation. The cost is not only emotional but economic.

Recognizing emotional labor subsidies allows you to stop internalizing outcomes that are not yours to manage. When you release responsibility for other people's feelings, reactions, or crises, you reclaim energy and attention. This shift restores balance and creates the mental clarity required for financial growth. Wealth flourishes when emotional labor is intentional, limited, and reciprocal.

Opportunity Costs: What Your Yes Prevents You From Choosing

Every yes automatically creates a no somewhere else, whether consciously or not. Opportunity cost is the invisible price you pay for choosing one path over another. When you say yes to low-impact commitments, you reduce your availability for higher-value opportunities. This often goes unnoticed because the lost opportunity is hypothetical, unseen, and unmeasured. Yet it is one of the most significant contributors to financial stagnation.

Obligation frequently disguises itself as necessity. "Family duty" can mask ongoing financial sacrifice that limits your independence. "Being a team player" can justify underpayment or overwork. "Exposure" often replaces real compensation with promises that never materialize. "Just helping out" becomes a recurring drain rather than a one-time gesture. Each of these narratives pressures you into saying yes while obscuring what you are giving up in return.

When opportunity cost is ignored, life becomes reactive instead of deliberate. You may feel loyal, helpful, and busy, yet increasingly disconnected from your own goals. The stress that follows is not confusion—it is your awareness signaling misalignment. Wealth requires discernment, and discernment requires the courage to decline what does not serve your long-term vision.

Learning to evaluate opportunity cost transforms decision-making. You begin to ask not only whether you can do something, but whether it is worth the trade. This shift moves you from survival mode into design mode. Wealth grows when your yes is reserved for what aligns, pays, and compounds over time.

Exercises:

Exercise 1: The Yes Audit

Step 1: Write down every recurring commitment, obligation, or responsibility you currently say yes to.

Step 2: Next to each item, note whether it provides financial return, emotional fulfillment, or neither.

Step 3: Identify which commitments drain time, energy, or emotional resources without meaningful return.

Step 4: Circle the top three that cause the most stress or stagnation.

Step 5: Reflect on which of these you agreed to out of obligation rather than choice.

Exercise 2: Obligation Translation

Step 1: List situations where you feel pressured to say yes.

Step 2: Write the phrase used to justify the obligation, such as "family duty" or "being helpful."

Step 3: Translate each phrase into its actual cost in time, energy, or money.

Step 4: Ask yourself whether this cost aligns with your current financial goals.

Step 5: Decide whether this obligation deserves continued access to your resources.

Exercise 3: Opportunity Cost Mapping

Step 1: Choose one recent yes that consumed significant time or energy.

Step 2: List three things you could not do because of that commitment.

Step 3: Identify which of those alternatives had the potential to improve your finances or well-being.

Step 4: Acknowledge the trade you made, without judgment.

Step 5: Commit to evaluating opportunity cost before your next major yes.

Power of No Advice Tip

Saying no is not a rejection of people; it is a protection of your future. When you decline intentionally, you prevent resentment from building and burnout from taking root. Clear refusals reduce confusion and eliminate unspoken expectations. The more calmly you say no, the less explanation is required. Consistency teaches others how to treat your time and energy. Boundaries create predictability, which lowers stress for everyone involved. Financial stability depends on decisions made from clarity, not guilt. Every no strengthens your ability to choose wisely.

Using the Power of No to Your Advantage

Using no strategically allows you to concentrate effort where it produces the highest return. When you reduce unnecessary commitments, your focus sharpens and your confidence grows. People begin to value your time more when access is limited. Opportunities that remain after you filter become more aligned and better compensated. Saying no early prevents costly entanglements later. Your schedule becomes intentional rather than reactive. Stress decreases as control increases. Wealth grows when your decisions are guided by purpose instead of pressure.

Journal Prompts

1. Where am I saying yes out of fear rather than alignment?
2. Which commitments feel heavy but unrewarding?
3. How has guilt influenced my financial decisions?
4. What does my time say about my priorities?
5. Where do I feel resentment building due to obligation?
6. Which yeses have cost me opportunities I cared about?
7. What would change if I protected my energy more fiercely?
8. How do I feel when I imagine saying no without explanation?
9. What obligations no longer fit who I am becoming?
10. What would a financially aligned yes look like for me?

Closing Reflection

Saying yes has been framed as kindness, loyalty, and responsibility, but unchecked yeses quietly erode stability and self-trust. When you recognize how time leaks, energy drains, emotional labor subsidies, and opportunity costs operate in your life, the problem becomes clear and actionable. You are not broken, lazy, or unmotivated—you are overextended. Naming the true cost of your yeses shifts the narrative from self-blame to self-awareness. From this place, saying no becomes an act of clarity rather than defiance. This chapter marks the beginning of reclaiming your resources, your agency, and your path toward sustainable wealth.

Chapter 2: The Financial and Psychological Benefits of Boundaries

The Trauma Loop: How Fear Quietly Destroys Wealth

The cycle begins with fear, often long before money is even mentioned. Fear of rejection, fear of conflict, fear of being seen as selfish, or fear of abandonment conditions the body to seek safety through compliance. Saying yes becomes a reflex, not a decision. In the moment, the yes feels relieving because it temporarily reduces tension. But relief is not resolution, and the nervous system remembers the cost.

After the yes comes resentment, even if it is subtle or denied. Resentment forms when your internal needs are overridden to protect someone else's comfort. This resentment drains emotional energy and corrodes motivation, making even simple tasks feel heavy. Over time, resentment transforms into burnout, where exhaustion becomes chronic and recovery becomes incomplete. Burnout then constrains earning capacity by limiting focus, creativity, and resilience.

Financial instability emerges not because of poor work ethic, but because the system is unsustainable. A person stuck in this loop is constantly reacting rather than designing, constantly compensating rather than investing. Decisions are made to avoid discomfort instead of to build stability. Money becomes associated with stress and obligation, reinforcing the original fear that triggered the loop.

Recognizing this trauma loop breaks its power. When you see that fear—not laziness or irresponsibility—is driving your financial patterns, self-blame dissolves. Boundaries interrupt the loop at its origin by replacing reflexive yeses with conscious choice. Wealth becomes possible when fear is no longer the primary decision-maker.

Generosity Versus Self-Betrayal: A Crucial Distinction

Generosity is often praised without examining its cost. True generosity expands both the giver and the receiver, leaving neither depleted. Self-betrayal, by contrast, feels like generosity on the surface but creates resentment, exhaustion, and quiet anger underneath. The difference is not intention, but consent. When generosity is chosen freely, it nourishes. When it is coerced internally, it corrodes.

Chosen generosity arises from clarity rather than pressure. You give because you want to, not because you feel you must. Resourced generosity means you give from surplus, not scarcity. It does not require sacrifice of stability, rest, or security. Time-bound generosity has a clear beginning and end, preventing it from becoming an open-ended drain.

Self-betrayal ignores these conditions. It says yes when resources are thin, when time is limited, or when the cost is unsustainable. It confuses endurance with virtue and martyrdom with morality. Over time, this pattern erodes self-trust, making it harder to say yes even when you want to. The result is emotional shutdown and financial stagnation.

Learning to distinguish generosity from self-betrayal restores balance. You begin to give without resentment and receive without guilt. Boundaries do not eliminate generosity; they refine it. Wealth grows when giving is intentional, limited, and aligned rather than automatic and draining.

Guilt Is Conditioned, Not Moral

Guilt often feels like an internal alarm, signaling wrongdoing. In reality, much financial guilt is learned rather than innate. It is conditioned through family systems, workplaces, cultures, and survival environments that reward compliance and punish refusal. Over time, the body associates saying no with danger, even when no real threat exists.

This conditioning creates a false moral narrative: that prioritizing yourself is wrong, that rest must be earned, and that money should be sacrificed for approval. These beliefs are reinforced through repetition, not truth. The discomfort you feel when setting a boundary is not evidence of harm; it is evidence of reprogramming. The nervous system is adjusting to a new rule set.

When guilt is mistaken for morality, it overrides logic. You may know a decision is financially unsound, yet still comply to relieve internal pressure. This keeps you trapped in cycles of overgiving and underearning. The body seeks short-term relief at the expense of long-term stability. Boundaries challenge this pattern by teaching the nervous system that discomfort does not equal danger.

As guilt loses its authority, clarity returns. Decisions become calmer, slower, and more deliberate. You learn to tolerate the sensation of discomfort without interpreting it as failure. This tolerance is a psychological asset that directly supports financial growth. Wealth expands when guilt no longer controls choice.

Boundaries as Safety, Not Separation

Many people fear that boundaries will isolate them or damage relationships. In truth, boundaries create safety by making interactions predictable and sustainable. When expectations are clear, resentment decreases and trust increases. Financially, this stability allows for long-term planning rather than constant crisis management.

Boundaries protect income by preventing chronic overextension. They preserve energy so that effort can be applied where it matters most. Psychologically, boundaries reduce anxiety by eliminating ambiguity and unspoken obligations. The mind relaxes when it knows what is required and what is not. This calm is essential for strategic thinking and wise decision-making.

Boundaries also retrain the nervous system to associate self-protection with safety. Each time you say no and survive the discomfort, the body learns a new lesson. The fear response weakens, and confidence strengthens. Over time, saying no becomes neutral rather than threatening.

When boundaries are internalized as safety mechanisms, wealth becomes less stressful to pursue. Money is no longer earned through depletion but through alignment. The result is a calmer, more resilient relationship with both work and worth.

Exercises:

Exercise 1: Trauma Loop Awareness

Step 1: Recall a recent situation where you said yes despite hesitation.

Step 2: Identify the fear that preceded the yes.

Step 3: Notice any resentment or exhaustion that followed.

Step 4: Observe how this affected your motivation or finances.

Step 5: Write one alternative boundary you could try next time.

Exercise 2: Generosity Check

Step 1: List recent acts of giving involving time, money, or energy.

Step 2: Mark whether each was chosen freely or felt pressured.

Step 3: Identify which acts left you resourced versus depleted.

Step 4: Redefine generosity for yourself using chosen, resourced, and time-bound criteria.

Step 5: Commit to giving only within those boundaries.

Exercise 3: Guilt Reframing

Step 1: Write down situations where guilt influences your financial choices.

Step 2: Identify where you learned this guilt.

Step 3: Separate the sensation of discomfort from actual harm.

Step 4: Practice sitting with the discomfort without acting on it.

Step 5: Reflect on how this changes your sense of control.

Power of No Advice Tip

Discomfort is not danger, even when it feels intense. Your body may react to boundaries as if something terrible is happening, but this is conditioning, not truth. Pause before responding to requests that trigger guilt. Give yourself time to assess whether a yes is aligned or habitual. Remember that urgency often serves others, not you. Calm refusals reduce emotional escalation. Over time, your nervous system will recalibrate. Boundaries become easier with repetition. Financial clarity grows when fear loses authority.

Using the Power of No to Your Advantage

Saying no strategically interrupts patterns that drain both money and energy. It allows you to choose generosity rather than perform it. Each no strengthens self-trust, making future decisions clearer. As fear decreases, creativity and confidence increase. Opportunities improve when access to you is selective. Your financial life becomes proactive instead of reactive. Stress decreases as stability increases. Wealth grows when your resources are protected first.

Journal Prompts

1. Where do I confuse guilt with morality?
2. How has fear shaped my financial decisions?
3. When does generosity become self-betrayal for me?
4. What discomfort am I avoiding by saying yes?
5. How does my body react when I consider saying no?
6. What beliefs about money and worth did I inherit?
7. How would my finances change with stronger boundaries?
8. Where do I need to redefine generosity?
9. What does safety feel like when I protect myself?
10. How can I practice tolerating discomfort this week?

Closing Reflection

Boundaries are not barriers to connection; they are foundations for stability. When you understand the trauma loop driving fear-based yeses, the cycle loses its grip. Separating generosity from self-betrayal restores integrity to both giving and receiving. Guilt, once recognized as conditioned, no longer dictates your choices. Discomfort becomes a signal of growth rather than danger. This chapter marks a shift from survival-driven decisions to intentional ones. As boundaries strengthen, so does your capacity for calm, clarity, and sustainable wealth.

Chapter 3: How to Say No to Bad Deals, Toxic People, and Low-Paying Work

Why Saying No Feels Harder Than Saying Yes

For many people, the difficulty of saying no is not intellectual—it is physiological. The body has learned that refusal leads to conflict, loss, or punishment, so it reacts with anxiety before words even form. This reaction creates urgency to soften the boundary, explain the decision, or retreat entirely. As a result, many noes never fully land; they dissolve into excuses, apologies, or conditional yeses that reopen negotiation.

Bad deals, toxic people, and low-paying work exploit this reflex. They thrive on ambiguity and hesitation, sensing when a boundary is unstable. When you overexplain, you unintentionally invite debate. Each justification becomes an opening for persuasion, pressure, or guilt. The conversation shifts from a decision to a negotiation, leaving you drained and exposed.

Understanding this dynamic reframes the problem. The issue is not that you lack assertiveness; it is that your nervous system associates clarity with danger. Saying no without collapse requires retraining both language and posture. Boundaries must be communicated simply and calmly to feel real to both you and others.

When no becomes a complete sentence, power returns to you. Clarity reduces emotional labor and prevents entanglement. Wealth and well-being grow when decisions are final rather than fragile.

Short, Calm, and Non-Defensive Refusals

Effective refusals are brief, steady, and free of emotional charge. Short refusals limit exposure and reduce the chance of manipulation. Calm refusals signal confidence and self-trust, even when discomfort is present. Non-defensive refusals communicate that no justification is required. Together, these qualities form a refusal that is both respectful and firm.

A short refusal might sound simple, but its simplicity is what makes it powerful. It does not invite argument or explanation. Calm delivery keeps the nervous system regulated, preventing escalation. Non-defensive tone avoids framing the boundary as a reaction or accusation. The message remains focused on the decision, not the relationship.

Bad deals often unravel when met with clarity. Toxic people lose leverage when emotional hooks are removed. Low-paying work becomes easier to decline when you stop framing refusal as a failure or betrayal. Each refusal reinforces the truth that your time and energy are valuable.

Practicing these refusals builds embodied confidence. The body learns that boundaries do not result in catastrophe. Over time, clarity replaces anxiety, and refusal becomes a neutral act rather than a dramatic one.

The Rule of Explanation and Negotiability

There is a direct relationship between explanation and vulnerability. The more you explain, the more negotiable your boundary becomes. Explanations provide material for persuasion, debate, and guilt-tripping. They shift the focus from your decision to your reasoning, which others may attempt to dismantle.

This rule applies in professional, personal, and financial contexts. When you justify your no, you imply that approval is needed. This undermines the boundary and places control outside of you. A clear no, offered without explanation, communicates finality. It signals that the decision has already been made.

Explanation is often used as a safety strategy. It feels polite, reasonable, and protective. In reality, it prolongs discomfort and increases emotional labor. Boundaries are most effective when they are simple and direct. Clarity is not cruelty; it is efficiency.

Learning to tolerate the silence after a no is essential. Silence is where confidence consolidates. When you stop filling space with justifications, your boundaries gain weight and credibility.

Collapse Responses and How to Prevent Them

Collapse responses occur when the nervous system overrides intention. Apologizing weakens the boundary by implying wrongdoing. Backtracking reopens negotiation and undermines trust in your words. Over-accommodating adds conditions that dilute the refusal. These responses are automatic for many people, especially those conditioned to prioritize harmony over self-protection.

Recognizing collapse responses allows you to interrupt them. Awareness creates a pause where choice can return. Instead of apologizing, you can restate the boundary. Instead of backtracking, you can hold silence. Instead of over-accommodating, you can end the conversation.

Bad deals often persist because collapse responses are predictable. When you eliminate these patterns, the dynamic shifts. People adjust when they realize the boundary is stable. Confidence grows as you witness your own resilience.

Preventing collapse is not about perfection; it is about practice. Each time you hold a boundary without collapse, your nervous system recalibrates. Strength becomes embodied rather than forced.

Exercises:

Exercise 1: Boundary Language Practice

Step 1: Write three short refusal statements you can use in different contexts.

Step 2: Remove all explanations and justifications.

Step 3: Practice saying each aloud with a calm tone.

Step 4: Notice physical sensations that arise.

Step 5: Repeat until the statements feel neutral.

Exercise 2: Collapse Awareness

Step 1: Recall a time you apologized after saying no.

Step 2: Identify what you feared in that moment.

Step 3: Rewrite the refusal without apology or explanation.

Step 4: Visualize holding the boundary calmly.

Step 5: Commit to using this version next time.

Exercise 3: Negotiation Interruption

Step 1: Identify situations where your no is often debated.

Step 2: Prepare a single sentence refusal.

Step 3: Practice ending the conversation after stating it.

Step 4: Resist the urge to fill silence.

Step 5: Reflect on how finality feels in your body.

Power of No Advice Tip

A refusal does not require emotional cushioning to be valid. Calmness communicates confidence more than explanation ever could. Silence after a no is not rudeness; it is completion. You are not responsible for managing others' disappointment. Each clear refusal strengthens your self-trust. Boundaries reduce stress by eliminating ambiguity. The body learns safety through repetition. Confidence grows when you stop negotiating with fear.

Using the Power of No to Your Advantage

Saying no cleanly saves time, energy, and emotional labor. It prevents entanglement in situations that drain resources. Each refusal reinforces your authority over your own decisions. Opportunities improve when access is selective. Stress decreases as clarity increases. Your reputation shifts toward reliability and strength. Wealth grows when effort is focused on aligned work. No becomes a tool for protection and progress.

Journal Prompts

1. Where do I overexplain my boundaries?
2. What do I fear will happen if I say no simply?
3. How does my body respond to silence after refusal?
4. When do I apologize unnecessarily?
5. What bad deals have I tolerated out of fear?
6. How can shorter refusals protect my energy?
7. What would confidence feel like in my body?
8. Where do I backtrack instead of holding firm?
9. How does clarity change my sense of control?
10. What boundary will I practice this week?

Closing Reflection

Learning to say no without collapse transforms boundaries from ideas into actions. When refusal becomes calm, brief, and non-defensive, it carries authority. Overexplaining fades as self-trust grows. Bad deals lose their grip, toxic dynamics dissolve, and underpaid work becomes easier to decline. This chapter shifts no from an emotional struggle into a practiced skill. With language and embodiment aligned, confidence becomes natural rather than forced. Wealth and stability follow when your boundaries finally hold.

Chapter 4: The Art of Selective Opportunities: Only Work on What Pays Big

Why Hustle Fails and Filters Win

Hustle culture teaches that success comes from doing more, saying yes faster, and staying perpetually busy. In reality, constant motion often hides a lack of direction. When everything is pursued, nothing is protected. Energy fragments, attention scatters, and income plateaus despite relentless effort. The problem is not a lack of ambition; it is the absence of filters.

Filters replace hustle with discernment. Instead of asking how much you can handle, filters ask what is worth handling at all. A filtered life reduces noise and increases signal. It conserves energy for work that compounds rather than drains. Wealth grows not from activity, but from alignment between effort and return.

When you operate without filters, you are forced to manage consequences later—missed deadlines, burnout, resentment, and financial stagnation. Wealthy individuals avoid this by declining early. Early noes are inexpensive; late noes are costly. Saying no at the beginning preserves time, reputation, and leverage.

Selective opportunity is not about being exclusive; it is about being intentional. Filters create a structure where your resources flow toward outcomes that matter. This shift marks the transition from survival-based work to strategic wealth building.

The Three Filters That Protect Income and Energy

Every opportunity should pass through three essential filters before receiving a yes. The first is compensation: does it pay enough for the time, skill, and energy required? If the answer is unclear or evasive, the opportunity is already misaligned. Adequate pay is not greed; it is sustainability. Underpaid work consumes the same energy as well-paid work while delivering less stability.

The second filter is scalability. Does this opportunity grow beyond your direct labor, or does it trap you in constant output? Scalable work compounds over time, increasing returns without proportionally increasing effort. Non-scalable work demands repeated energy for the same result. Wealth accumulates when effort produces expanding outcomes.

The third filter evaluates impact on energy. Does this opportunity drain you, or does it compound your capacity? Draining work leaves you depleted and reactive. Compounding work strengthens skills, confidence, and resources. Energy-aware decisions protect your nervous system, which directly affects clarity and performance.

Applying these filters consistently transforms decision-making. Opportunities become clearer, and pressure loses its influence. You begin choosing from strength rather than obligation. Income stabilizes as effort becomes focused and intentional.

Why Saying No Early Is a Wealth Skill

Wealthy people decline opportunities before they become problems. They do not wait for exhaustion or resentment to justify refusal. Early noes prevent entanglement and preserve optionality. This habit is not arrogance; it is risk management.

Late noes often involve explanations, apologies, and damage control. They cost emotional labor and sometimes reputation. Early noes are clean and quiet. They maintain relationships without sacrificing boundaries. This efficiency protects both energy and credibility.

Saying no early requires trusting your evaluation skills. It means honoring your filters even when an opportunity appears attractive on the surface. Wealth grows when decisions are based on criteria rather than emotion. Each early no sharpens discernment.

Over time, this practice reduces stress dramatically. Life becomes simpler as fewer commitments compete for attention. Financial growth accelerates when energy is not wasted managing misaligned obligations.

Fewer Projects, Cleaner Focus, Bigger Returns

More projects do not equal more progress. Each additional commitment divides attention and dilutes effectiveness. Fewer projects allow for deeper focus, higher quality output, and stronger results. Clean focus is a multiplier that turns effort into leverage.

When you reduce the number of active pursuits, decision fatigue decreases. Creativity improves because the mind is not constantly switching contexts. Financial returns increase because energy is concentrated where it produces the highest value. This is wealth by subtraction.

Bigger returns come from depth, not breadth. Mastery develops when focus is sustained. Relationships improve when presence is undivided. Opportunities improve when your reputation reflects selectivity and excellence.

Choosing fewer paths does not limit potential; it amplifies it. Selective opportunity creates space for rest, strategy, and growth. Wealth becomes a natural outcome of clarity rather than exhaustion.

Exercises

Exercise 1: Opportunity Filter Test

Step 1: Write down three current or recent opportunities.

Step 2: Evaluate whether each pays enough for the required effort.

Step 3: Assess whether each opportunity scales or repeats labor.

Step 4: Identify whether each drains or compounds energy.

Step 5: Decide which opportunities deserve continued access to your time.

Exercise 2: Early No Practice

Step 1: Identify an opportunity you feel pressured to accept.

Step 2: Apply the three filters honestly.

Step 3: Draft a short refusal statement.

Step 4: Practice delivering it calmly.

Step 5: Notice the relief created by early clarity.

Exercise 3: Subtraction Planning

Step 1: List all active projects or commitments.

Step 2: Rank them by financial return and energy impact.

Step 3: Identify one project to pause or exit.

Step 4: Reallocate freed time to a higher-value activity.

Step 5: Track changes in focus and stress levels.

Power of No Advice Tip

Not every opportunity deserves a response, and not every invitation deserves consideration. Early evaluation saves months of regret. Clear criteria remove emotion from decision-making. Saying no early is an act of respect for your future. Filters reduce pressure and confusion. Wealth favors those who choose deliberately. Less commitment creates more capacity. Strategic refusal is a form of discipline.

Using the Power of No to Your Advantage

Selective noes protect income by preventing underpaid work. They preserve energy for opportunities that compound. Focus sharpens when distractions are removed. Confidence grows as decisions align with values. Stress decreases as commitments simplify. Reputation improves through consistency and clarity. Wealth builds through intentional allocation of effort. No becomes a gateway to bigger returns.

Journal Prompts

1. Where am I overcommitted right now?
2. Which projects drain more than they return?
3. How do I feel when I imagine fewer commitments?
4. What filters do I currently use, if any?
5. Where do I delay saying no until it costs me?
6. What would change if I said no earlier?
7. How does focus affect my income?
8. What work truly compounds over time for me?
9. Where am I mistaking busyness for progress?
10. What would wealth by subtraction look like in my life?

Closing Reflection

Selective opportunity is the bridge between effort and wealth. When filters replace hustle, clarity replaces chaos. Saying no early preserves energy, reputation, and choice. Fewer projects create space for mastery, focus, and growth. Wealth no longer requires exhaustion; it requires discernment. This chapter marks the shift from chasing everything to choosing intentionally. From here, your yes becomes powerful because it is rare, deliberate, and aligned.

Chapter 5: Mastering "No" to Design Your Ideal Life

"No" as Identity: Who You Become When You Choose Yourself

When no becomes part of your identity, decisions stop being situational and start being coherent. You are no longer someone who evaluates every request emotionally; you are someone who knows who you are and what you protect. Identity-based boundaries remove negotiation from your self-worth. You stop asking, *Is it okay if I say no?* and start stating, *This is not aligned with who I am.* That shift alone changes how others perceive and treat you.

An identity-centered no is calm, consistent, and recognizable. People learn quickly where you stand, what you tolerate, and what you value. This consistency builds respect, even when disappointment is present. Respect grows not because everyone agrees with you, but because your boundaries are stable. Stability signals maturity, reliability, and self-leadership.

When no is internalized as identity, guilt loses leverage. You are no longer rejecting people; you are honoring your standards. This reframing dissolves the emotional chaos that once followed refusal. You no longer need to justify or soften your decisions because they are rooted in self-definition rather than mood.

Wealth responds to identity. Income increases when you operate from clarity rather than reactivity. Opportunities improve when people know your yes is intentional and rare. Designing your life begins with deciding who you are willing to be, and who you are no longer willing to perform for.

"No" as Lifestyle: How Boundaries Shape Daily Reality

A lifestyle built on intentional noes feels radically different from one built on constant accommodation. Your calendar breathes. Your days have margins. Rest becomes regular instead of accidental. This is not laziness; it is design. A protected lifestyle allows you to show up fully where it matters.

When no becomes a lifestyle practice, you stop living in anticipation of interruption. Time is no longer something you defend; it is something you allocate. Energy is no longer drained by constant decision-making. You begin each day with clarity instead of dread, knowing that your commitments were chosen, not imposed.

This lifestyle shift reduces stress at a structural level. Anxiety decreases because expectations are clear. Relationships stabilize because resentment fades. Work improves because focus deepens. Life feels less frantic and more intentional, even when challenges arise.

A boundary-based lifestyle is seen from the outside as calm and grounded. From the inside, it feels spacious and sustainable. This environment is where creativity, consistency, and wealth naturally grow. No becomes the architecture that holds your days together.

"No" as Wealth Architecture: Building a Life That Pays You Back

Wealth architecture is the intentional design of how money, time, and energy circulate in your life. Saying no is the structural beam that prevents collapse. Without it, income leaks through overextension, emotional labor, and misaligned commitments. With it, resources compound.

Intentional money decisions require protected time and regulated energy. When boundaries are weak, financial choices are rushed and reactive. When boundaries are strong, decisions are deliberate and strategic. Money becomes a tool rather than a stressor. You spend, save, and invest from clarity instead of pressure.

Wealth architecture prioritizes sustainability over intensity. It values consistency more than bursts of effort. Saying no to underpaying work, draining relationships, and chaotic environments preserves earning capacity. Over time, this creates upward momentum that exhaustion never could.

A well-designed financial life feels calm rather than frantic. Bills are handled with intention, not panic. Income grows because effort is focused. No is not an obstacle to wealth; it is the framework that makes wealth livable.

Closing the Arc: From Reactive Yes to Aligned Wealth

At the beginning of this journey, yes was a reflex. It was driven by fear, guilt, and survival. Each yes promised safety but delivered stress. Over time, it created a life that felt busy yet unstable, full yet unsatisfying. This was never a personal failure—it was a boundary gap.

Through practice, awareness, and repetition, no became intentional. It interrupted old patterns and created space for discernment. You learned to tolerate discomfort without interpreting it as danger. Decisions slowed down. Self-trust strengthened. Alignment replaced urgency.

Aligned wealth emerges when identity, lifestyle, and money are in agreement. Your work reflects your values. Your schedule supports your nervous system. Your finances reinforce your priorities. No holds the system together, ensuring that what you build does not consume you.

This is mastery—not perfection, but coherence. You are no longer chasing stability; you are designing it. No becomes the quiet force that protects everything you value.

Exercises

Exercise 1: Identity Alignment

Step 1: Write three values that define who you are becoming.

Step 2: List commitments that contradict those values.

Step 3: Identify one boundary that would realign your actions with your identity.

Step 4: Write a simple no that honors that identity.

Step 5: Commit to practicing it this week.

Exercise 2: Lifestyle Design Audit

Step 1: Review your weekly schedule.

Step 2: Mark activities that energize versus drain you.

Step 3: Identify one draining activity to remove or reduce.

Step 4: Replace it with rest, focus, or high-value work.

Step 5: Observe changes in stress and clarity.

Exercise 3: Wealth Architecture Mapping

Step 1: List your current income-related commitments.

Step 2: Evaluate which are aligned, scalable, and sustainable.

Step 3: Identify one that undermines your financial stability.

Step 4: Draft a boundary or exit plan.

Step 5: Reallocate energy toward a higher-alignment opportunity.

Power of No Advice Tip

Respect grows from consistency, not compliance. Each intentional no reinforces your standards. Boundaries make relationships clearer, not colder. Calm refusal builds trust over time. Wealth favors those who protect their capacity. No is an investment in sustainability. Loss is not in refusal but in overextension. Power comes from choosing deliberately.

Using the Power of No to Your Advantage

No allows you to curate your life instead of reacting to it. It protects time so focus can deepen. It preserves energy so effort compounds. It clarifies money decisions by removing pressure. Relationships improve as resentment fades. Confidence strengthens through repetition. Opportunities align with values. Wealth grows within a structure that supports you.

Journal Prompts

1. Who am I when I say no without guilt?
2. What identity am I ready to stop performing?
3. How does my ideal lifestyle feel on a daily basis?
4. Where does my current life contradict my values?
5. What would intentional wealth look like for me?
6. How does respect feel different from approval?
7. Where do I still equate no with loss?
8. What becomes possible when my time is protected?
9. How has my relationship with money changed through boundaries?
10. What kind of life am I now designing?

Closing Reflection

Mastering no is not about withdrawal; it is about authorship. When you stop reacting and start choosing, your life reorganizes around what matters. Respect replaces resentment, clarity replaces chaos, and alignment replaces exhaustion. No becomes the quiet structure holding your wealth, relationships, and peace in place. This is not the end of connection—it is the beginning of a life designed with intention.

Appendix A: The Ultimate Boundary-Setting Scripts

These scripts are not excuses.

They are **complete decisions delivered calmly**.

Each script is designed to:

- Protect time, energy, and income
- Prevent negotiation and guilt spirals
- Eliminate overexplaining and emotional collapse
- Reinforce respect through clarity

You may adapt the wording to your voice, but **do not dilute the structure**. The power of these scripts lies in their simplicity and finality.

Script 1: The Clean No (For Bad Deals, Requests, and Invitations)

Script:

"That doesn't work for me. I won't be moving forward with it."

This script is intentionally short. It communicates a decision without explanation, justification, or emotional cushioning. The absence of detail signals confidence and finality. It does not accuse, defend, or debate. It simply closes the door.

Many people feel compelled to add reasons after this line, especially when discomfort rises. Resist that urge. The moment you explain, you reopen negotiation. This script works precisely because it does not offer material for persuasion or pressure.

Use this script when declining low-paying work, misaligned opportunities, unpaid labor, or requests that do not deserve further discussion. It is neutral, respectful, and firm. Silence after delivering it is not rude—it is completion.

If pushback occurs, repeat the script verbatim. Repetition reinforces stability and teaches others that your boundaries are not flexible under pressure.

Script 2: The Professional No (For Work, Business, and Financial Situations)

Script:

"I've reviewed the details, and I'm not available for this opportunity."

This script communicates discernment rather than rejection. It signals that you considered the request and made an intentional choice. It does not invite counteroffers, emotional appeals, or urgency-based manipulation.

This script is especially effective in professional environments where politeness is expected but boundaries are often tested. It protects your reputation while preserving your authority. There is no apology because no wrongdoing occurred.

Avoid adding qualifiers such as "right now," "maybe later," or "if things change," unless you genuinely intend to reopen the conversation. Ambiguity weakens boundaries and increases follow-up pressure.

If asked for reasons, you may respond with:

"I'm focusing on other priorities."

Then stop. Your priorities do not require approval.

Script 3: The Relational No (For Family, Friends, and Emotional Requests)

Script:

"I care about you, but I'm not able to take this on."

This script separates care from compliance. It reassures connection without sacrificing boundaries. It prevents emotional manipulation by refusing responsibility for outcomes that are not yours to manage.

This script is especially important for emotionally loaded situations where guilt is often used to override self-protection. It acknowledges the relationship without absorbing the burden. Care does not mean capacity, and this script makes that distinction clear.

Do not follow this script with solutions, alternatives, or emotional labor unless you genuinely want to offer them. Over-accommodating after refusal undermines the boundary and reinforces dependency.

If the other person reacts emotionally, allow them to feel what they feel. Their emotions are not evidence that your boundary is wrong. This script holds space without surrendering stability.

Script 4: The Repeat and Close (For Pushback, Pressure, and Boundary Testing)

Script:

"I've already shared my decision, and it hasn't changed."

This script is used when someone attempts to renegotiate, guilt-trip, or wear you down after a clear no. It reinforces finality without escalation. It is calm, controlled, and non-defensive.

Boundary testing often escalates when people sense uncertainty. This script removes that uncertainty. It does not argue, persuade, or justify. It simply restates reality.

Use this script as many times as necessary, word for word. Consistency is more powerful than creativity. Each repetition strengthens your authority and weakens manipulation.

After delivering this script, you may end the conversation. Continuing to engage after restating a boundary teaches others that persistence works. Closure is part of enforcement.

How to Use These Scripts Effectively

- Choose the script **before** you are emotionally activated
- Deliver it **slowly and calmly**
- Stop speaking after the script
- Allow silence to do the work
- Repeat if necessary, without variation

These scripts are not tools for conflict—they are tools for **clarity**.

Closing Note

Boundaries are not proven through explanation; they are proven through consistency.

Each time you use these scripts, your nervous system learns that no is safe.

Each time you hold the line, respect increases—even if approval does not.

These scripts are not about pushing people away.

They are about **protecting the life you are building**.

Use them often.

Use them calmly.

And remember: the strongest boundary is the one you do not debate.

Message from the Author:

I hope you enjoyed this book, I love astrology and knew there was not a book such as this out on the shelf. I love metaphysical items as well. Please check out my other books:

-Life of Government Benefits

-My life of Hell

-My life with Hydrocephalus

-Red Sky

-World Domination:Woman's rule

-World Domination:Woman's Rule 2: The War

-Life and Banishment of Apophis: book 1

-The Kidney Friendly Diet

-The Ultimate Hemp Cookbook

-Creating a Dispensary(legally)

-Cleanliness throughout life: the importance of showering from childhood to adulthood.

-Strong Roots: The Risks of Overcoddling children

-Hemp Horoscopes: Cosmic Insights and Earthly Healing

- Celestial Hemp Navigating the Zodiac: Through the Green Cosmos

-Astrological Hemp: Aligning The Stars with Earth's Ancient Herb

-The Astrological Guide to Hemp: Stars, Signs, and Sacred Leaves

-Green Growth: Innovative Marketing Strategies for your Hemp Products and Dispensary

-Cosmic Cannabis

-Astrological Munchies

-Henry The Hemp

-Zodiacal Roots: The Astrological Soul Of Hemp

- **Green Constellations: Intersection of Hemp and Zodiac**

-Hemp in The Houses: An astrological Adventure Through The Cannabis Galaxy

-Galactic Ganja Guide

Heavenly Hemp
Zodiac Leaves
Doctor Who Astrology
Cannastrology
Stellar Satvias and Cosmic Indicas
Celestial Cannabis: A Zodiac Journey
AstroHerbology: The Sky and The Soil: Volume 1
AstroHerbology:Celestial Cannabis:Volume 2
Cosmic Cannabis Cultivation
The Starry Guide to Herbal Harmony: Volume 1
The Starry Guide to Herbal Harmony: Cannabis Universe: Volume 2
Yugioh Astrology: Astrological Guide to Deck, Duels and more
Nightmare Mansion: Echoes of The Abyss
Nightmare Mansion 2: Legacy of Shadows
Nightmare Mansion 3: Shadows of the Forgotten
Nightmare Mansion 4: Echoes of the Damned
The Life and Banishment of Apophis: Book 2
Nightmare Mansion: Halls of Despair
Healing with Herb: Cannabis and Hydrocephalus
Planetary Pot: Aligning with Astrological Herbs: Volume 1
Fast Track to Freedom: 30 Days to Financial Independence Using AI, Assets, and Agile Hustles
Cosmic Hemp Pathways
How to Become Financially Free in 30 Days: 10,000 Paths to Prosperity
Zodiacal Herbage: Astrological Insights: Volume 1
Nightmare Mansion: Whispers in the Walls
The Daleks Invade Atlantis
Henry the hemp and Hydrocephalus

10X The Kidney Friendly Diet
Cannabis Universe: Adult coloring book

Hemp Astrology: The Healing Power of the Stars

Zodiacal Herbage: Astrological Insights: Cannabis Universe: Volume 2

Planetary Pot: Aligning with Astrological Herbs: Cannabis Universes: Volume 2

Doctor Who: Convergence Protocol – The Replicator War

Nightmare Mansion: Curse of the Blood Moon

The Celestial Stoner: A Guide to the Zodiac

Cosmic Pleasures: Sex Toy Astrology for Every Sign

Hydrocephalus Astrology: Navigating the Stars and Healing Waters

Lapis and the Mischievous Chocolate Bar

Celestial Positions: Sexual Astrology for Every Sign

Apophis's Shadow Work Journal: **:** A Journey of Self-Discovery and Healing

Kinky Cosmos: Sexual Kink Astrology for Every Sign

Digital Cosmos: The Astrological Digimon Compendium

Stellar Seeds: The Cosmic Guide to Growing with Astrology

Apophis's Daily Gratitude Journal

Cat Astrology: Feline Mysteries of the Cosmos

The Cosmic Kama Sutra: An Astrological Guide to Sexual Positions

Unleash Your Potential: A Guided Journal Powered by AI Insights

Whispers of the Enchanted Grove

Cosmic Pleasures: An Astrological Guide to Sexual Kinks

369, 12 Manifestation Journal

Whisper of the nocturne journal(blank journal for writing or drawing)

The Boogey Book

Locked In Reflection: A Chastity Journey Through Locktober

Generating Wealth Quickly:How to Generate $100,000 in 24 Hours

Star Magic: Harness the Power of the Universe

The Flatulence Chronicles: A Fart Journal for Self-Discovery

The Doctor and The Death Moth

Seize the Day: A Personal Seizure Tracking Journal

The Ultimate Boogeyman Safari: A Journey into the Boogie World and Beyond

Whispers of Samhain: 1,000 Spells of Love, Luck, and Lunar Magic: Samhain Spell Book

Apophis's guides:Witch's Spellbook Crafting Guide for Halloween

Frost & Flame: The Enchanted Yule Grimoire of 1000 Winter Spells

The Ultimate Boogey Goo Guide & Spooky Activities for Halloween Fun

Harmony of the Scales: A Libra's Spellcraft for Balance and Beauty

The Enchanted Advent: 36 Days of Christmas Wonders

Nightmare Mansion: The Labyrinth of Screams

Harvest of Enchantment: 1,000 Spells of Gratitude, Love, and Fortune for Thanksgiving

The Boogey Chronicles: A Journal of Nightly Encounters and Shadowy Secrets

The 12 Days of Financial Freedom: A Step-by-Step Christmas Countdown to Transform Your Finances

Sigil of the Eternal Spiral Blank Journal

A Christmas Feast: Timeless Recipes for Every Meal

Holiday Stress-Free Solutions: A Survival Guide to Thriving During the Festive Season

Yu-Gi-Oh! Holiday Gifting Mastery: The Ultimate Guide for Fans and Newcomers Alike

Holiday Harmony: A Hydrocephalus Survival Guide for the Festive Season

Celestial Craft: The Witch's Almanac for 2025 – A Cosmic Guide to Manifestations, Moons, and Mystical Events

Doctor Who: The Toymaker's Winter Wonderland

Tulsa King Unveiled: A Thrilling Guide to Stallone's Mafia Masterpiece

Pendulum Craft: A Complete Guide to Crafting and Using Personalized Divination Tools

Nightmare Mansion: Santa's Eternal Eve

Starlight Noel: A Cosmic Journey through Christmas Mysteries

The Dark Architect: Unlocking the Blueprint of Existence

Surviving the Embrace: The Ultimate Guide to Encounters with The Hugging Molly

The Enchanted Codex: Secrets of the Craft for Witches, Wiccans, and Pagans

Harvest of Gratitude: A Complete Thanksgiving Guide

Yuletide Essentials: A Complete Guide to an Authentic and Magical Christmas

Celestial Smokes: A Cosmic Guide to Cigars and Astrology

Living in Balance: A Comprehensive Survival Guide to Thriving with Diabetes Insipidus

Cosmic Symbiosis: The Venom Zodiac Chronicles

The Cursed Paw of Ambition

Cosmic Symbiosis: The Astrological Venom Journal

Celestial Wonders Unfold: A Stargazer's Guide to the Cosmos (2024-2029)

The Ultimate Black Friday Prepper's Guide: Mastering Shopping Strategies and Savings

Cosmic Sales: The Astrological Guide to Black Friday Shopping

Legends of the Corn Mother and Other Harvest Myths

Whispers of the Harvest: The Corn Mother's Journal

The Evergreen Spellbook

The Doctor Meets the Boogeyman

The White Witch of Rose Hall's SpellBook

The Gingerbread Golem's Shadow: A Study in Sweet Darkness

The Gingerbread Golem Codex: An Academic Exploration of Sweet Myths

The Gingerbread Golem Grimoire: Sweet Magicks and Spells for the Festive Witch

The Curse of the Gingerbread Golem

10-minute Christmas Crafts for kids

Christmas Crisis Solutions: The Ultimate Last-Minute Survival Guide

Gingerbread Golem Recipes: Holiday Treats with a Magical Twist

The Infinite Key: Unlocking Mystical Secrets of the Ages

Enchanted Yule: A Wiccan and Pagan Guide to a Magical and Memorable Season

Dinosaurs of Power: Unlocking Ancient Magick

Astro-Dinos: The Cosmic Guide to Prehistoric Wisdom

Gallifrey's Yule Logs: A Festive Doctor Who Cookbook

The Dino Grimoire: Secrets of Prehistoric Magick

The Gift They Never Knew They Needed

The Gingerbread Golem's Culinary Alchemy: Enchanting Recipes for a Sweetly Dark Feast

A Time Lord Christmas: Holiday Adventures with the Doctor

Krampusproofing Your Home: Defensive Strategies for Yule

Silent Frights: A Collection of Christmas Creepypastas to Chill Your Bones

Santa Raptor's Jolly Carnage: A Dino-Claus Christmas Tale

Prehistoric Palettes: A Dino Wicca Coloring Journey

The Christmas Wishkeeper Chronicles

The Starlight Sleigh: A Holiday Journey

Elf Secrets: The True Magic of the North Pole

Candy Cane Conjurations

Cooking with Kids: Recipes Under 20 Minutes

Doctor Who: The TARDIS Confiscation

The Anxiety First Aid Kit: Quick Tools to Calm Your Mind

Frosty Whispers: A Winter's Tale

The Infinite Key: Unlocking the Secrets to Prosperity, Resilience, and Purpose

The Grasping Void: Why You'll Regret This Purchase

Astrology for Busy Bees: Star Signs Simplified

The Instant Focus Formula: Cut Through the Noise

The Secret Language of Colors: Unlocking the Emotional Codes

Sacred Fossil Chronicles: Blank Journal

The Christmas Cottage Miracle

Feeding Frenzy: Graboid-Inspired Recipes

Manifest in Minutes: The Quick Law of Attraction Guide

The Symbiote Chronicles: Doctor Who's Venomous Journey

Think Tiny, Grow Big: The Minimalist Mindset

The Energy Key: Unlocking Limitless Motivation

New Year, New Magic: Manifesting Your Best Year Yet

Unstoppable You: Mastering Confidence in Minutes

Infinite Energy: The Secret to Never Feeling Drained

Lightning Focus: Mastering the Art of Productivity in a Distracted World

Saturnalia Manifestation Magick: A Guide to Unlocking Abundance During the Solstice

Graboids and Garland: The Ultimate Tremors-Themed Christmas Guide

12 Nights of Holiday Magic

The Power of Pause: 60-Second Mindfulness Practices

The Quick Reset: How to Reclaim Your Life After Burnout

The Shadow Eater: A Tale of Despair and Survival

The Micro-Mastery Method: Transform Your Skills in Just Minutes a Day

Reclaiming Time: How to Live More by Doing Less

Chronovore: The Eternal Nexus

The Mind Reset: Unlocking Your Inner Peace in a Chaotic World
Confidence Code: Building Unshakable Self-Belief
Baby the Vampire Terrier
Baby the Vampire Terrier's Christmas Adventure
Celestial Streams: The Content Creator's Astrology Manual
The Wealth Whisperer: Unlocking Abundance with Everyday Actions
The Energy Equation: Maximize Your Output Without Burning Out
The Happiness Algorithm: Science-Backed Steps to Joyful Living
Stress-Free Success: Achieving Goals Without Anxiety
Mindful Wealth: The New Blueprint for Financial Freedom
The Festive Flavors of New Year: A Culinary Celebration
The Master's Gambit: Keys of Eternal Power
Shadowed Secrets: Groundhog Day Mysteries
Beneath the Burrow: Lessons from the Groundhog
Spring's Whispers: The Groundhog's Prediction
The Limitless Mindset: Unlock Your Untapped Potential
The Focus Funnel: How to Cut Through Chaos and Get Results
Bold Moves: Building Courage to Live on Your Terms
The Daily Shift: Simple Practices for Lasting Transformation
The Quarter-Life Reset: Thriving in Your 20s and 30s
The Art of Shadowplay: Building Your Own Personal Myth
The Eternal Loop: Finding Purpose in Repetition
Burrowing Wisdom: Life Lessons from the Groundhog
Shadow Work: A Groundhog Day Perspective
Love in Bloom: 5-Minute Romantic Gestures
The Shadowspell Codex: Secrets of Forbidden Magick
The Burnout Cure: Finding Balance in a Busy World
The Groundhog Prophecy: Unlocking Seasonal Secrets
Nog Tales: The Spirited History of Eggnog
Six More Weeks: Embracing Seasonal Transitions
The Lumivian Chronicles: Fragments of the Fifth Dimension

Money on Your Mind: A Beginner's Guide to Wealth
The Focus Fix: Breaking Through Distraction
January's Spirit Keepers: Mystical Protectors of the Cold
Creativity Unchained: Unlocking Your Wildest Ideas in 2025
Manifestation Mastery: 365 Days to Rewrite Your Reality
The Groundhog's Mirror: Reflecting on Change
The Weeping Angels' Christmas Curse
Burrowed in Time: A Groundhog Day Journey
Heartbeats: Poems to Share with Your Valentine
Dino Wicca: The Sacred Grimoire of Prehistoric Magick
Courage of the Pride: Finding Your Inner Roar
The Lion's Leap: Bold Moves for Big Results
Healthy Hustle: Achieving Without Overworking
Practical Manifesting: Turning Dreams into Reality in 2025
Jurassic Pharaohs: Unlocking the Magick of Ancient Egypt and Dino Wicca
The Happiness Equation: Small Changes for Big Joy
The Confidence Compass: Finding Your Inner Strength
Whispers in the Hollow: Tales of the Forgotten Beasts
Echoes from the Hollow: The Return of Forgotten Beasts
The Hollow Ascendant: The Rise of the Forgotten Beasts
The Relationship Reset: Building Better Connections
Mastering the Morning: How to Win the Day Before 8 AM
The Shadow's Dance: Groundhog Day Symbolism
Cupid's Kitchen: Quick Valentine's Day Recipes
Valentine's Day on a Budget: Love Without Breaking the Bank
Astrocraft: Aligning the Stars in the World of Minecraft
Forecasting Life: Groundhog Day Reflections

Bleeding Hearts: Twisted Tales of Valentine's Terror

Herbal Smoke Revolution: The Ultimate Guide to Nature's Cigarette Alternative

Winter's Wrath: The Complete Survival Blueprint for Extreme Freezes.

The Groundhog's Shadow: A Tale of Seasons
Burrowed Insights: Wisdom from the Groundhog
Sensual Strings: The Art of Erotic Bondage
Whispered Flames: Unlocking the Power of Fire Play
Forgotten Shadows: A Guide to Cryptids Lost to Time
Six Weeks of Secrets: Groundhog Day's Hidden Messages
Shadows and Cycles: Groundhog Day Reflections
The Art of Love Letters: Crafting the Perfect Message
Romantic Getaways at Home: Turning Your Space into Paradise
Purrfect Brews: A Cat Lover's Guide to Coffee and Companionship
The Groundhog's Wisdom: Timeless Lessons for Modern Life
The Shadow Oracle: Groundhog Day as a Predictor
Emerging from the Burrow: A Journey of Renewal
The Language of Love: Learning Your Partner's Love Style
Authorpreneur: The Ultimate Blueprint for Writing, Publishing, and Thriving as an Author
Weathering the Seasons: Groundhog Day Perspectives
Valentine's Day Magic: A Guide to Romantic Rituals
The Shadow Chronicles: Stories of Groundhog Day
Love and Laughter: Fun Games for Valentine's Day
AstroRealty: Unlocking the Stars for Property Success
The Groundhog's Path: A Guide to Seasonal Balance
Groundhog Day Diaries: Reflections in the Shadow
The Groundhog's Light: Illuminating the Path Ahead
Valentine's Traditions from Around the World
AI Wealth Revolution: Unlocking the Trillionaire Mindset
Love Rekindled: Reigniting Passion in Relationships
Single and Thriving: Self-Love on Valentine's Day
Emerald Legends: Mystical Tales of Ireland
Green Alchemy: Harnessing Nature's Magic
The Hearts of Horror: A Valentine's Day Nightmare

The Leprechaun's Guide to Wealth and Wisdom
Dancing with the Sidhe: Celebrating the Otherworld
Shamrocks and Shadows: Mysteries of the Green Isle
Emerald Energy: Harnessing Luck and Growth
The Gingerbread Golem's Valentine: A Sweetheart's Guide to Love and Enchantment
The Celtic Knot: Weaving Life and Destiny
Green Fire: Elemental Magic for St. Patrick's Day
Clover Chronicles: Finding Your Inner Luck
Ireland's Mystical Creatures: A Field Guide
Gingerbread Golem's Love Almanac
Prowl and Thrive: The Lion's Guide to Success
Love Alchemy: Transforming Your Life Through Heart Energy
WORLD DOMINATION: Woman's Rule 3:The New Life
The Midnight Rose: A Guide to Lunar Love Spells
The Forbidden Letters: Writing Your Own Love Prophecy
Luck and Lore: St. Patrick's Day for Modern Mystics
The Green Path: A Pagan Celebration of Renewal
The Dark Architect's Guide to Reprogramming Reality
Prankster's Paradise: A Guide to Harmless Hijinks
Manifest Your Reality: The Law of Attraction Simplified
The TARDIS Owner's Manual: Understanding the Doctor's Ship: *A complete guide to the TARDIS, its technology, secrets, and mysteries*
Starlit Romance: Astrology Secrets for Finding True Love
The Time Lord's Atlas: A Complete Guide to the Whoniverse: ***A breakdown of the locations, planets, and dimensions explored in Doctor Who***
Sweetheart Shadows: The Dark Side of Love and Attraction
February Fire: Reigniting Passion in Every Area of Life
The Self-Love Toolkit: 5 Ways to Embrace Who You Are
February Sparks: Ignite Your Dreams in 28 Days

March to Success: A 31-Day Action Blueprint
Ancient Paths: The 13 Sacred Principles of Dino Wicca
Echoes of Tomorrow: Navigating the AI Revolution
The Wellness Blueprint: Balancing Mind, Body, and Soul
Green Horizons: Sustainable Living for a Better Tomorrow
The AI Wealth Code: How to Make Millions with Automation
AI-Powered Creativity: Writing, Art, and Music for Profit
Extinction Rites: Rebirthing Your Soul Through Prehistoric Magick
Sacred Serpents tarot
Celestial Enchantment blank journal
Star Strains
Culinary Journeys: Exploring Global Flavors at Home
The Hollowvale Curse
The Hollowvale Harvest
The Egg of Transformation: Awakening Your Inner Power
Blooming Into Power: A Wiccan Guide to Spring Awakening
The Nightmare Nexus: The Third Doctor's Perilous Haunting
Digital Detox: Reclaiming Your Life in a Connected World
Ostara's Path: Walking the Spiral of Renewal
The Sacred Hare
Financial Freedom: Building Wealth in the Modern Age
Spring's Cauldron: Stirring the Waters of Change
The Hollowvale Pact
Quantum Consciousness: The Science of Reality Shifting
The Hollowvale Hunger
The Sacred Waters Within: A Witch's Guide to Hydrocephalus Magick
The Raven's Nest: Building a Life of Unshakable Stability
AI and the Human Mind: The Future of Intelligence
The Hollowvale Reckoning
Timeless Love: Building and Maintaining Lasting Relationships

The Raven's Roar: Unlocking Unstoppable Confidence
Raven Sight: Awakening Intuition and Inner Wisdom
The Butterfly Effect: Small Changes, Big Transformations
Taming the Boogeyman: How to Conquer Your Inner Fears
The Magick of Green: Awakening Earth's Energy in You
The Entrepreneurial Mindset: Secrets to Business Success
The Hollowvale End
The Shadow Luck Ritual: Reclaiming Power from Your Dark Side
Spring Magick for Beginners: A Simple Guide to Seasonal Energy Work
Doctor Who: The Hollowvale Conundrum
The March of Miracles: Unlocking Synchronicities in Spring
Unveiling the Cosmos: A Guide to Stargazing and Space Exploration
The Ultimate Guide to Surviving an Economic Collapse
The AI Gold Rush: How to Profit from the AI Revolution
Bastet's Shadow: The Hidden Power of Feline Magick
The Bastet Codex: Unlocking the Goddess's Magickal Secrets
Purring Spells: Harnessing Bastet's Healing Frequencies
Bastet's Nine Lives: Rebirth, Transformation, and Immortality Spells
Primal Currents: Hydrocephalus Magick in the Path of Dino Wicca
The Digital Gold Rush: Mastering E-Commerce and Online Sales
Future Shock: Adapting to the Next Decade of Change
The Quantum Mindset: Think Like a Billionaire
Sacred Motherhood: Awakening the Divine Feminine Within
The Mother's Spellbook: Enchantments for Love, Protection, and Prosperity
The Witch's Guide to Parenting: Raising Empowered and Intuitive Children

The Magick of Motherhood: Reclaiming Your Power Through Rituals
The Pagan Path to Self-Love: A Goddess's Guide to Worth and Confidence
Wild Woman Magick: Unleashing Your Primal Power
The Money Magnet Blueprint: Unlocking Unlimited Wealth
Biohacking 101: Unlock Your Body's Full Potential
The Wild Father: A Pagan Guide to Strength and Wisdom
The Sacred Masculine: Unlocking Your Inner Power
The Druid's Compass
The Warrior's Mindset
The Father's Fire
Odin's Path
Ancestral Bonds
The House That Whispers
The Magician's Code
The Wild Hunt
The Green Man's Path
The Altar of Success
The Shadow and the Sword
The High Priestess's Guide to Energy Healing
The Lunar Mother
The Sacred Self-Care Grimoire
The Womb Wisdom Codex
The Wheel of the Mother
The Witch's Guide to Manifestation
The Q2 Reset
The Ultimate Guide to AI-Powered Passive Income
Escape the 9-5
AI Feline Fortunes
The Tear-Stained Grimoire
Razorblade Runes
Cemetery Sirens

The Midnight Wristwatch
The Town That Forgets
AI Horror & Creepypasta
The Hollow Frequency
The Breach Echo
The Quiet Between Worlds
The Sigil of Tharan-Khul
Summon the Vault of Y'ha'ten
The Becoming Codex
The Profit of Az'ra-nar
The Drowned Logos
Echoes of the Eldritch Will
The Deep Ledger
Necronomicon of Networth
Covenant of the Wealthwyrm
The Whisperer's Manifesto
The Rites of Azh-K'luth
The Ark of the Crawling Coin
The Tithe of Shadows
Inkheart Abyss
The Timewinds of Y'ha-nthlei
The Spiral Labyrinth of Azag-Nirrh
The Gallifreyan Heresy of the Black Pharaoh
The Psalms of Nyog-Sotha
Black Rain Alchemy
The Infinite Maw
The Entropic Blueprint
The Oracle of Sh'guul
The Book of Breach
The Drowned Saint's Testament
Dreamcraft of the Sleeper God
The Silence Market
Cthonomics: The Dark Wealth Algorithm

Invocation of the Ten-Eyed King
Wealthbound to the Wyrm Below
Become the Unnameable
Codex of the Sovereign Flame
Rituals of Relentless Becoming
The Shadow Ascends
The Eyes Beneath You
The Will That Wakes Worlds
Silence Is a Weapon
The Mirror That Screams
The Whisper Between Moments
The Mind That Devours Fear
The Myth of the Finished Self
The Architect of Your Madness
The Voice You've Buried
The Discipline of Madness
Stormborn: Awakening Your Inner Tempest
The Mind That Ate Time
Unbind Your Becoming
The Pact You Owe Yourself
The Devourer's Diet
The Acid That Carves the Path
The Tower You Must Burn
The Breath Between Worlds
Speak Like the Deep
The Labyrinth Within
The Spine of the Sea God
Rejection Is a Portal
The Crown You Refused
The Scar Is the Spell
The Lightless Flame
The Habit of Becoming Horrific
ChickenJockey Chaos

The Gatekeeper Within
You Are Not Your Name
The Compass of the Mad
The Archive of Unsent Letters
What the Mirror Can't Show You
The Knife You Needed
Worship Nothing, Become Everything
The Other Voice
The Body the World Forgot
The Vein of the Void
The Black Bone Codex
The Puzzle of the Hidden Self (Millennium Puzzle)
The Eye That Sees the Lie *(Millennium Eye)*
The Ring of Return (Millennium Ring)
The Rod of Relentless Will ***(Millennium Rod)***
The Tally of the Soul (Millennium Tauk/Necklace)
The Key to the Locked Timeline (Millennium Key)
The Scale of Sacred Decisions (Millennium Scales)
Inferno Bites: The UnOfficial Minecraft Lava Cookbook
Rot in the Attic
Prana: The Hidden Force of Your Infinite Self
The Shadow Realm Within: Transforming Darkness Into Destiny
The Borderland Collapse
Claws of Protection: Bastet's Defensive Magick
Mr. Ring-a-Ding's Madness
Yugioh Astrology: Celestial Deckcraft and Duel Destiny (2026–2027 Edition)
The Seal You Signed: Unlocking the Power You Once Feared
The Puzzle of Infinite Minds: Unlocking the Mentalism Hidden Within
The Eye That Mirrors the All: Secrets of Inner Reflection
Doctor Who: The Toymaker's Broadcast

The Rod of Eternal Flow: Commanding the Currents of Vibration
Golden Eyes of Bastet: Enhancing Psychic Vision
The Key of Dual Forces: Balance Within the Polarity
The Scales of Living Rhythm: Timing the Dance of Life
The Necklace of Hidden Cause: Weaving the Webs of Fate
The Ring of Secret Masters: Rising Through the All Within All
Daggers of the Dying Deep
Bastet's Wealth and Fortune Magick: Prosperity Rituals of the Goddess
The Tide that Speaks
The Scrolls of Petosiris: 13 Rituals from the Feathered Eye
Petosiris and the Living Plague of Osirion
Feline Fire: Bastet's Passion and Love Magick
The Star Altar of Petosiris
Bastet's Whiskers: Supernatural Sensory Magick
The Bastet Grimoire
Feeding the Shadows
The Mouthless Prayer
The Spiral Wound
Becoming the Ibis: Lessons from Petosiris's Mind
The Crimson Coven: Cola Magick for Sweet Dominion
Sacred Cat's Paw
The Soda Zodiac: A Flavor for Every Sign
Covenant of the Crawling Flame
The Ink of Ish'Zur
Frothroot: The Thirst That Ate the World
The Golden Glyphs of Prosperity
The Etherbind Codex
Echoes of the Resistance: Reclaiming the You That Survived
Harnessed Minds: Breaking Free from Mental Control
The Eyes in the Smoke

Rootwake: The Carbon Covenant
Skitter Logic: Unlearning the Fear That Built You
Doctor Who: The World That Froths
Rootwake: The Fizz That Rewrites Flesh
Rootwake: Frothfather of the World
The Holly Pact: Blood Beneath the Mistletoe
The 2nd Mass Principle: Building Unbreakable Tribes
Web of Wits: A Survival Guide to Encounters with Anasi the Spider (Aunt Nancy)
The Hexbreaking Handbook: Effective Spells to Remove Curses
Pop Alchemy: Transform Your Life One Sip at a Time
The Mason Code: Leading in Unleadable Times
Petosiris and the Fifth Chamber of Thoth
The Ether Seed Within
The Parent of Tomorrow
Petosiris's Pyramid of Perpetual Wealth
Unlearn the World
Grimoire of the Hollow Tongue
Zodiac Weeds: Finding Your Strain Through the Stars
Aquarius Rises in the Bank
The Sugar God's Smile
The Skinclock Reversal: Biohacking the Face of Time
Debtburn: How to Obliterate What You Owe Forever
The Ice Cream Oracle: What Your Cone Says About Your Future
Silence Is Sovereignty: The Power of Being Unreadable
The Wind That Whispers Through Stone
Path of the Four Directions
Doctor Who: The Maestro's Symphony of Endings
Oxygen Grail: Breathing to Undo the Clock
Zodiacal Collapse: When Stars Devour Time
Teachings from the Red Sand Silence

Doctor Who: Omega – The Broken Equation
Memory Wipe Your Past: Start Over Like a MiB
Mitochondria Prime: Ignite the Core of Youth
A Nest of Roaches
Grub from the Galaxy: MiB Recipes You'll Never Forget
Whiskers of Power: Bastet's Guide to Inner Sovereignty
The Gift Must Cost Them: Negotiation Through Unequal Exchange
The Worm Guys' Wealth Code: Hustle Like an Alien
Bug Out: The Edgar Method for Ruthless Goal Setting
Weaving Life with Spiderwoman's Pattern
Doctor Who: The Rani's Renaissance
How to Get a Job (If You're a Puppygirl)
Speak Through Others: The Art of Proxy Power
T-Rex Your Trauma: Reclaim the Power of Your Primal Self
The Black Briefcase: How MiB Stay Wealthy in Silence
The Thirst Beyond Reason: Understanding Diabetes Insipidus From the Inside Out
Backwoods Witchcraft for Billionaires: The Pagan Path from Dirt Roads to Gold Roads
The Moonshine Grimoire: Fermented Spells for Abundance
The Nameless Geometry
The Wraith's Mixtape: Spellcasting with Songs of Sorrow
The Gallifreyan Gentleman: Silent Wealth, Sonic Confidence, and the Doctor's Code of Living
Sugar Water Confidence
Dino Totems: Spirit Guides from Earth's First Gods
Pumpkin Sigils & Ritual Smoke
The Hózhó Compass
The Distortus Discipline – Order from Inner Mutation
Witchcraft for the Cold-Blooded Soul
Moonlight Over the Blessingway
Water, Interrupted: When the Body Forgets How to Hold On

Deformed but Divine: Embracing Your Asymmetry
Hexes in the Henhouse: The Farm Witch's Guide to Power
The Reversed Flame: A Grimoire of Inverted Power
Salt, Cells, and Sanity: Reclaiming Balance with Diabetes Insipidus
King of the Broken: Crowning the Flawed Self
Moonlight Scars: Emo Moon Magick and the Art of Lunar Sorrow
Noose Spells: Magick of the Hanging Rope
The Goth Cathedral: Rituals of the Broken and Beautiful
The Cretaceous Codex: Dino Spirits and Fossil Magick
The Turkey Bones Ritual
Nine Lives of Manifestation: Unlocking Bastet's Reality Codes
Chaos Muscles: Building Strength from Twisted Pain
Emo Blood Magick: The Veins of Power
The 3AM Flood: Nighttime Urination, Sleep Loss, and the DI Spiral
The Silence Between the Stars
The Lemon Method: Sour Your Way to Success
Starlit Sovereign
The Rite of Twelve Gates: Walking the Gates of the Duat.
Cornbread and Conjure: Recipes for Riches and Rootwork
The Black Rose Rituals: Emo Love Spells and Obsession Magick
The Eternal Goodbye: Death Magick and Rebirth Rituals
Sinkrot: The Drain That Remembers
The Hybrid Mindset: Thinking Beyond Evolution
Bone Dry: Navigating Dehydration Before It Breaks You
Wreathcraft: Winter Sigils and Yuletide Spells
The Rite of Twelve Mouths
S'mores of the Damned: Haunted Recipes for Halloween Night

Rethink the Drink: A Beverage Survival Guide for DI Warriors

The Shadow Chord: Guitar Magick and Sonic

Malformed Yet Majestic: Leading When You Feel Wrong Inside

The Cursed Diary: Ink-Stained Spells of the Emo Soul

Anxiety Off Switch: Emergency Reset for a Fried Nervous System

The Energy Heist: How to Take Back Your Life from Drainers

Beyond the Bathroom: Rebuilding Your Social Life With DI

Coyote's Gift for Decision Makers

Ghoul-Goo: Spooky S'mores You'll Die For

Echoes in the Mirror: Scrying and Self-Destruction Magick

Thread and Thorn: Stitching Spells from Rural Cloth

The Mogwai Mind: Building Untouchable Wealth from Small Ideas

Be Your Own Guide: Trust Your Inner Compass

Hormones in Chaos: The Endocrine Puzzle of Diabetes Insipidus

ChronoCleanse: Detox Your Biological Timeline

The Limb You Hide Is the One That Saves You

Leaves, Bones, and Whisper Spells

The Dinosaur Mindset: Prehistoric Tactics for Modern Wealth

Clawing Back Control: A Bastet Method for Boundaries and Empowerment

Samhain Codes of the Forgotten

Orange Alchemy: The Autumnal Spellbook

Monster Within, Master Without

The Sigil That Sleeps

Hearthcraft: Yule Hearth Sigils and Winter Warmth Spells

Temple of the Purring Moon: Rituals from Bastet's Lineage

When the Earth Remembers Your Footsteps

Food for Mood: Eat to Heal Depression, Not Just Survive It
Witch of the Kudzu Vine: Southern Pagan Wealth Secrets
The Invisible Diagnosis: Advocating for Yourself With DI
The Coffin's Lullaby: Sleep Magick and Nightmares as Portals
Ashes of the Will: Rituals for Erasing the Self
The Fracture Rite: Shattering the Magickal Core
Funeral Candles: The Art of Emo Flame Magick
The Black Grimoire: A Blank Ritual for Writing in Absence
Phantom Thirst: A Halloween Survival Guide for Diabetes Insipidus
The Hollow Crown: Emo Royalty and Magick of the Outcast King
Sandpainting for the Soul
Falling Into Balance: Using the Extra Hour to Recalibrate Life
100 Southern Superstitions That Still Work
The DI Child: A Parent's Guide to Raising Hydrated, Happy Kids
The Jungle of Shame: Escaping the Hidden Lab of Doubt
The Witch's Toast: S'mores Spells and Creepy Confections
The Hoodoo Pantry: Spells from the Mason Jar
The Immortal Fortune: Secret Wealth Lessons from Captain Jack Harkness
The Specter's Embrace: Magick for Channeling Ghostly Lovers
Grateful Waters: A Thanksgiving Survival Guide for Diabetes Insipidus
The Seizure Gospel
Harvestbind: Autumn Sigils and Samhain Spells
Doctor Who: The Algorithmic Awakening
Silent Nights, Steady Waters: A Christmas Survival Guide for Diabetes Insipidus
The Extra Hour Effect: How One Hour Can Transform Everything

Blade Between the Breaths

Running with the Mountain Shadows

Echoes of the Failed Experiment – Becoming a Living Legacy

Swamp Witches & River Ghosts: Real Southern Hauntings

Cornbread Prophecies: Magical Recipes from a Southern Table

Doctor Who: The Signal in the Star

Bloomcraft: Spring Sigils and Equinox Enchantments

Vanisher: How to Disappear from the Internet Without Losing Your Life

The Ultimate Christmas Cookie Cookbook

The Unbreakable Parent: How to Mentally Survive Raising Kids in a Broken World

Time Debt: How to Reclaim the Hours You Didn't Know You Lost

One Month, One Million: Unconventional Cash Creation Tactics

Doctor Who: The Cyber Conversion Protocol

Black Friday Frenzy: The Art of Finding Hidden Online Deals

The Grimoire Buried Under the Apple Tree

Digital Couponing Masterclass: Your Step-by-Step Guide to Black Friday Savings

The Fire Inside the Flint

Shadows on the Ceiling: The Emo Guide to Astral Magick

The Bone-Eaters Beneath Us

Black Friday Bundle Blueprint: Creating Irresistible Product Packages for Maximum Sales

Thirteen Nights of Unbinding

Doctor Who: Engines of Influence

Pumpkin Spice Alchemy: Recipes of Fire and Frost

When Raptor Met Rexy: Prehistoric Lessons in Wild Romance

Oblivion's Candle: Burn the Path Behind You

Campfire Curses and Chocolate: A Halloween S'mores Grimoire
The Wallet That Wasn't Mine: Breaking Free from Inherited Scarcity
The Cola Zodiac: What Your Fizz Says About Your Fate
Frostfire Fortune: Unlocking Winter's Hidden Prosperity
Signal Jamming: Detox Your Brain from Info Overload
The Dust of the Forgotten Rite
The Golden Cat Sigils: Drawing Power in Bastet's Name
Mud Magick: The Prosperity of Getting Dirty
Savory Spicefall: Beyond the Pumpkin Pie
Pumpkin Spice Apothecary Kitchen
The Pumpkin Spice Economy: Turning Trends into Billions
The Ember Veil: 13 Nights of Fire Magick
Financial Freeze: When Earning Triggers Panic
The Gingerbread Alchemist: Sweet Recipes with a Twist
Biosynth Power: Programming Yourself from Scratch
Echoes from the Talking Circle
Truffle Alchemy: Fungus of Fortune
Spores of Power: The Truffle Witch's Handbook
Doctor Who: The Tower That Speaks
The Mycelium Veil: Truffle Magick Unbound
Broke But Ashamed: Healing the Shame Wound of Debt
The Evergreen Mind: Growth Through Winter Stillness
The Black Veil Truffle Rite
The Voice Beneath Symbols
Witchlight on the Bayou: Swamp Spells for Sovereignty
I Grew Up Poor and Now I Sabotage My Success
The Lantern of Hollow Souls
Shutdown Survival: A Citizen's Guide to Thriving When Government Stops
When Abundance Feels Like a Threat: Healing the Hidden Fears of Enough

The Scarecrow Grimoire
Owls of the October Veil
Candlewax and Curses: A Halloween Spellbook
Excavating the Inner Fossil – Transforming Fossilized Thoughtforms into Tools of Power
The Yule Witch's Spellbook: Magick for the Holiday Season
Haunted Christmas: Ghost Stories for Winter Nights
The Christmas Survival Guide: Thriving Through the Chaos
The Bone Orchard Rites
Haunted Commerce: The Ghost in the Marketplace
When Money Triggers the Inner Child
Silent Night with the Silence: A Christmas Thriller
The Lightning Crown: Living and Leading Through Seizures
TARDIS Tidings: Festive Stories from the Whoniverse
Autumn Reset: Slowing Down Without Falling Behind
The Trillion Dollar Soul: Rewriting the Currency of Reality
Truffle Eclipse Magick
Micro-Manifestations: Quick Magick That Works
5-Minute Rituals for Busy Witches
The Marshmallow Massacre: Halloween Treats with a Sinister Twist
Blood and Blackberry Thorns
Magickal Mornings: Rituals for a Blessed Christmas Day
Embers of the All-Hallows Fire
The Pumpkin Market Collapse
The Hour You Gained: Transforming Time Into Power
The Chamber Must Be Sealed: Mastering the Power of Controlled Access
The Cursed Manuscript of Petosiris
The Festive Hearth: Creating Holiday Traditions
Darkness Rising: Thriving as Nights Grow Longer
Harvesting Time: Turning the Year's End Into Your New Beginning

Petosiris and the 13th Zodiac Key
Wagewound: When Paychecks Become Identity Prisons
Walls That Watch
The Silent Feast: Rituals of Power in the Longest Night
The Distortus Legacy : Becoming a Deformed King in a Perfect World
The Hollow Masks
The Gratitude Furnace: Forging Gold from Thanks
Feast of Inner Gold: Eating for Energy and Enlightenment
Haunted Commerce: The Season of Spending Spirits
Fear Bonds: How Panic Creates Profit
Black Friday E-Commerce Playbook: Sales Tactics to Skyrocket Your Holiday Revenue
Budgeting for Black Friday: A Holiday Savings Planner
Haunting the Harvest Moon
The Warrior's Water: Emergency Preparedness for People With DI
The First Sip of the Year: A New Year's Survival Guide for Diabetes Insipidus
Doctor Who: The Thirteenth Node
The Unseen Struggle: Mental Health, Anxiety, and Chronic Thirst
The Hearth's Hidden Ledger: Counting Energies as Currency
The Gift Alchemist: Turning Any Offering Into Gold
The Papyrus of the Bound Spirit
The Magick of Leftovers: Transmutation in the Fridge
Frost and Fortune: Christmas Wealthcraft for the Modern Magus
Last-Minute Gifts: Creative Ideas on a Budget
10 Secrets to Surviving Holiday Crowds
The Witch's Dow Jones
The Witches' Graveyard Shift
Pumpkin Sigils: Carving Rites for Midnight Power

The Secret Shopper's Black Friday Guide: How to Get Early Access and VIP Deals

Fever in the Foundation

The Neuralyzer Reset: Reprogram Your Morning Routine

Lightning Lessons of the White Painted Woman

The Enchanted Snowflake

The Magic Sip: Surviving Disney Parks with Diabetes Insipidus

The One Who Draws Through You

Santa's Secrets: A Magical Holiday Planner

Silent Bells, Loud Miracles: Self-Help for the Season of Stillness

The Sugar Spell Codex: Confectionary Magick of Christmas

Autumn Hexcraft: Fallen Leaves, Fallen Barriers

Sleep Like a Fortress: Build a Life Where Insomnia Can't Survive

Nowhere Was Ever Home

Christmas Under the Stars: A Celestial Holiday Guide

Rentproof: How to Never Be Evicted Again

Workless: Escape the 9-5 Without Being Broke

The Gilded Gift: A Wealth Altar for Christmas Morning

The Black Friday Grimoire

The Hollowing: Ceremonies of Spiritual Collapse

Doctor Who: The Nameless Signal

Where the Eagle Hides His Courage

The Dwarf Tyrant's Ascent: Claiming Power in a World of Giants

The Currency of the Dead: Trading with Spectral Bankers

The Icebound Witch: Survival and Magick in the Cold

The Emergency Money Mind: Constant Crisis, Zero Calm

Thirst & Roses: A Valentine's Survival Guide for Diabetes Insipidus

Springing Into Clarity: Mastering the Energy Shift of Daylight Saving

Speed of the Nanotyrant: Agile Strategies for Life's Hunt

The 90-Day Reset: A Science-Backed Guide to Reinvent Yourself Before the New Year

The Coil of Thorns

Timegates Unleashed

Dopamine Fasting 2.0: Rewiring Your Brain in a World of Overstimulation

The Nanotyrannus Mutation: Embracing Your Differentiated Form

Unwritten January: How to Use the Blank Page of the Year to Re-Author Your Life

Feast of the Forgotten Spirits: Ancestor Magick for the Holidays

The Burnout Codex: A System for Thriving Beyond Stress

I Don't Deserve to Have Money

When the King Doesn't See You: The Shadow Predator's Guide

The Reset Ritual :A Guide to Shedding Last Year's Weight—Emotional and Physical—by Spring Cleaning Your Soul

Calendar Alchemy: Learn to Bend Time and Productivity around Your Natural Rhythms

The Mirror Contract: A One-Sentence Agreement with Yourself that Unlocks Real Change

The Nile Formula: Sacred Flow for Millionaire Minds

Forward Momentum: Productivity Rituals for the Lost Hour

Harvest Gold: Wealth Magick of Pumpkin Spice Commerce

The Magick of Christmas Lights: Illuminating Holiday Rituals

Cranberry Crown: Royal Self-Worth through Ritual Meals

Petosiris and the Worms of the Feathered Throne

The Evergreen Equation: Self-Help for Sustained Growth

The Rain Will Wash Us Away: Emo Weather Magick

Snowlight Shadows: Magick Under Frozen Stars

Doctor Who: Merger of Empires

The Light Within the Feast: Magickal Wealth of Yuletide Flame

Momentum Machines: Small Habits Designed to Snowball into Unstoppable Forward Motion

Calm Spells: Magickal Solutions for Anxiety Relief

Santa's Final List: The Naughty Never Leave

The Mystic's Guide to Banishing Worry

The Silence Dividend: Turning Quiet Mornings into Compounding Growth All Year

Charmed Stillness: Rituals to Ease the Mind

Blood Spiral Ascension

The Vanishing Heart Invocation

Crystal Calm: Harnessing Stones for Anxiety

The Nano Tyrant Code: Strength in the Small Predator

The Energy Ledger: Accounting Methods for Vitality, Not Just Money

Snowglobe Mindset: Shake Up Your Thoughts, Settle Into Peace

The Weight of the Feather: Anubis's Codes for Soul Balance

Pocket Peppermint Power: Tiny Rituals for Big Holiday Energy

Shadowkeeper of the Golden Jackal: Anubis's Path to Energetic Protection

The Witch's Breath: Anxiety Relief Through Magickal Breathing

The Tiny Ember: Pocket Motivation for Cold Days

Stocking Sorcery: Mini Spells for Holiday Luck and Prosperity

Warm Hands, Steady Heart: Micro Grounding for Winter Anxiety

The Jackal's Lantern: Guide-Lights for Walking the Dark Path

Anubis's Silent Steps: Rituals for Stealth, Peace & Emotional Quiet

The Bonewake Protocol

Extinction-Proof: How to Outlive Trends, Trauma, and Time

The Fourth Doctor: The Eccentric Wanderer

The Second Doctor: Chaos and Charm in the TARDIS (Patrick Troughton, 1966–1969)

The Third Doctor: Earthbound Defender of Time (Jon Pertwee, 1970–1974)

The First Doctor: Genesis of the Time Lord (William Hartnell, 1963–1966)

The Fourth Doctor: The Eccentric Wanderer ***(Tom Baker, 1974–1981)***

The Fifth Doctor: Elegance and Empathy (Peter Davison, 1982–1984)

The Sixth Doctor: A Kaleidoscope of Conflict (Colin Baker, 1984–1986)

The Seventh Doctor: The Strategist of Shadows (Sylvester McCoy, 1987–1989)

The Eighth Doctor: A Time Lord's Renaissance (Paul McGann, 1996)

The War Doctor: A Time Lord's Burden (John Hurt, 2013)

The Ninth Doctor: The Healer of Worlds

(Christopher Eccleston, 2005)

The Tenth Doctor: The Lonely Hero (David Tennant, 2005–2010)

The Eleventh Doctor: The Madman in a Box (Matt Smith, 2010–2013)

The Twelfth Doctor: The Rebel with a Cause (Peter Capaldi, 2013–2017)

The Thirteenth Doctor: Breaking the Mold

(Jodie Whittaker, 2017–2022)

The Fourteenth Doctor: A New Beginning (David Tennant, 2022–2023)

The Fifteenth Doctor: Rewriting the Stars

(Ncuti Gatwa, 2023–2025)

Santa's Shortcut to Success: Micro Habits for a Better New Year

The Midnight Cocoa Manifesto: Comfort Rituals for Hard Nights

Why I Can't Save: Trauma Blocks to Financial Planning

Dino Brain, Mega Goals: Rewire Yourself for Savage Success.

Jurassic Profit: Unearth Your Inner Millionaire Fossil

Scales & Softness: Dating with Dino Heart

Carnotaurus Dreams.

Red Willow Thinking.

Reindeer Resilience: How to Keep Going When You're Exhausted

Candlewick Courage: Lighting Strength in Dark Seasons.

Elf-Mode Focus: Fast Attention Fixes for Busy Seasons

Futureproof Feelings: Emotional Skill-Building for Resilience No Matter What the New Year Brings

The 90-Day Rewire: Transform Your Neural Pathways Before Spring Blooms

Jolly Rich: Christmas Micro-Money Magick for Fast Prosperity.

Gingerbread Gratitude: Mini Practices for a Happier Holiday

Trauma-Spending: When Money Becomes a Drug

Goal Skeletons: Build Minimalist Frameworks for Resolutions That Last

The Snarl Strategy: Growling Back at a World That Silenced You

The Hourglass Reset: Reclaiming What the Clock Took

Yule Claw: Dino Rites of Light in the Darkness

Sacred Circles: Grounding Rituals for Anxious Souls

Clockstopper's Gut: Rebuilding the Core of Time

Winterfire Drive: Harness the Cold Season's Stillness to Ignite Deep Motivation

The 5-Minute Productivity Hack: Small Steps to Big Results

Light Ascending: A Self-Help Guide to Longer Days

Inner Economy: Trade Self-Doubt for Confidence Like a High-Value Currency

Simple Success: Decluttering Your Life for Better Results

The Resilient Mind: Thriving in Tough Times

The 2026 Playbook: Mastering the Year Ahead

The Spring Sleep Solution: Conquering Fatigue After Time Change.

The Hormonal Compass: Navigate Back to Your Youth

Golden Vision: Eating for Your Eye Color with the Power of Ghee

Lionhearted Love: Strength in Relationships

MiB Mindset: Think Like a Cosmic Agent

The Ladder of Small Wins: Climb Out of Stagnation by Stacking Micro-Victories

The Momentum Hour: Gaining More in Less Time.

The Year of You: A Self-Help Blueprint for Unapologetic Self-Ownership

The Dust That Watches You Back.

The Astral Parent

Shadow of the King: The Nanotyrannus Parable

Tiny Tidings of Triumph: Small Wins That Change Your Life

Dwarf Tyrant Rising: When You're the One They Overlook

The Bank Account Mirror: Healing How You See Yourself Through Money

Cretaceous Black

When Love Costs Too Much: Romantic Triggers and Financial Wounds

Dream-Eater's Guide to Wealth

Unzipped Reality: The Jacket That Opens Portals

Get Some Tarot cards: https://www.makeplayingcards.com/sell/apophis-occult-shop

Get some shirts: https://www.bonfire.com/store/apophis-shirt-emporium/

Instagrams:
@apophis_enterprises,
@apophisbookemporium,
@apophisscardshop
Twitter: @apophisenterpr1
Tiktok:@apophisenterprise
Youtube: @sg1fan23477
Hive: @sg1fan23477
CheeLee: @SG1fan23477

Podcast: Apophis Chat Zone: https://open.spotify.com/show/5zXbrCLEV2xzCp8ybrfHsk?si=fb4d4fdbdce44dec

Newsletter: https://apophiss-newsletter-27c897.beehiiv.com/

If you want to support me or see posts of other projects that I have come over to: **buymeacoffee.com/mpetchinskg**

I post there daily several times a day

Get your Dinowicca or Christmas themed digital products, especially Santa Raptor songs and other musics. Here: **https://sg1fan23477.gumroad.com**

Apophis Yuletide Digital has not only digital Christmas items, but it will have all things with Dinowicca as well as other Digital products.

www.ingramcontent.com/pod-product-compliance
Lightning Source LLC
LaVergne TN
LVHW022008200926
848481LV00007B/2288